B

STUDENT BO

¿Amazing English!™

AN INTEGRATED ESL CURRICULUM

Addison-Wesley Publishing Company

ISBN 0-201-85367-1
1 2 3 4 5 6 7 8 9 10-BAM-99 98 97 96 95

CONTENTS

New Friends

Hello, friends.
Hóla, amigos.
Allo, zanmi.

Welcome to school!

HELLO, AMIGOS

EXCERPTED FROM THE BOOK BY TRICIA BROWN
PHOTOGRAPHS BY FRAN ORTIZ

Hello, amigos!
My name is Frankie Valdez.

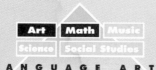

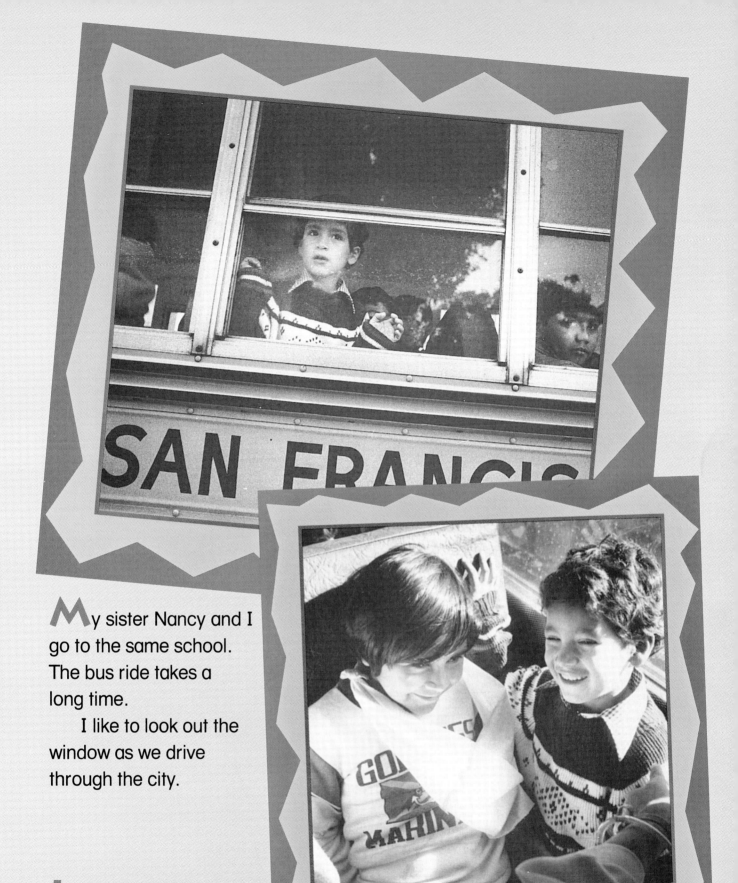

My sister Nancy and I go to the same school. The bus ride takes a long time.

I like to look out the window as we drive through the city.

I always sit with my best friend, Marvin Martinez.

New Friends

At my school the first and second graders are in the same classroom.

Some of us speak Spanish at home, and we learn English here at school.

Our first lesson is math. Sometimes I don't get it.

6

Mrs. Giddings, my teacher, helps me to understand. She speaks Spanish, too.

After recess we study English. I like English best when I get the right answer.

My Day/Mi Día

EXCERPTED FROM THE BOOK BY REBECCA EMBERLEY

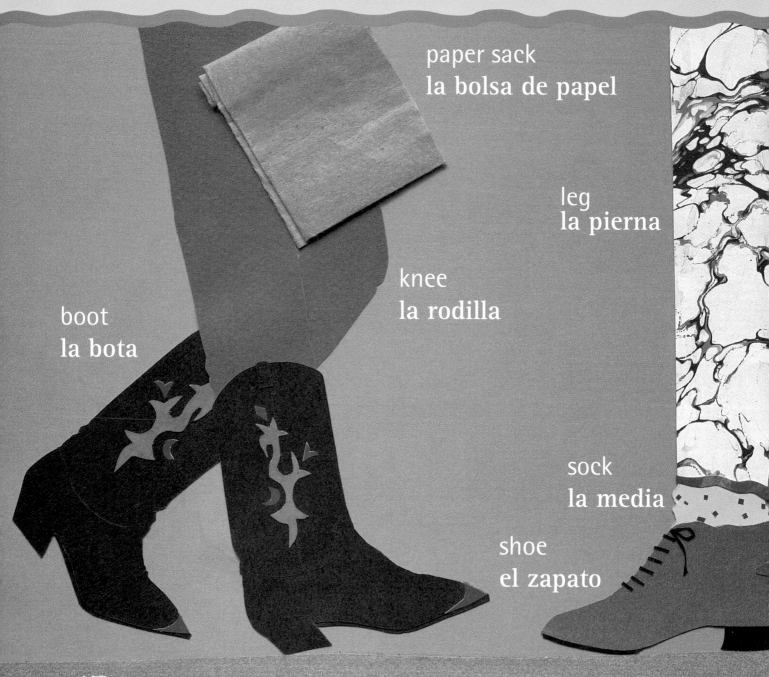

paper sack
la bolsa de papel

leg
la pierna

knee
la rodilla

boot
la bota

sock
la media

shoe
el zapato

I walk to school with my friends.
Camino a la escuela con mis amigos.

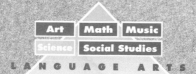

Art · Math · Music
Science · Social Studies

LANGUAGE ARTS

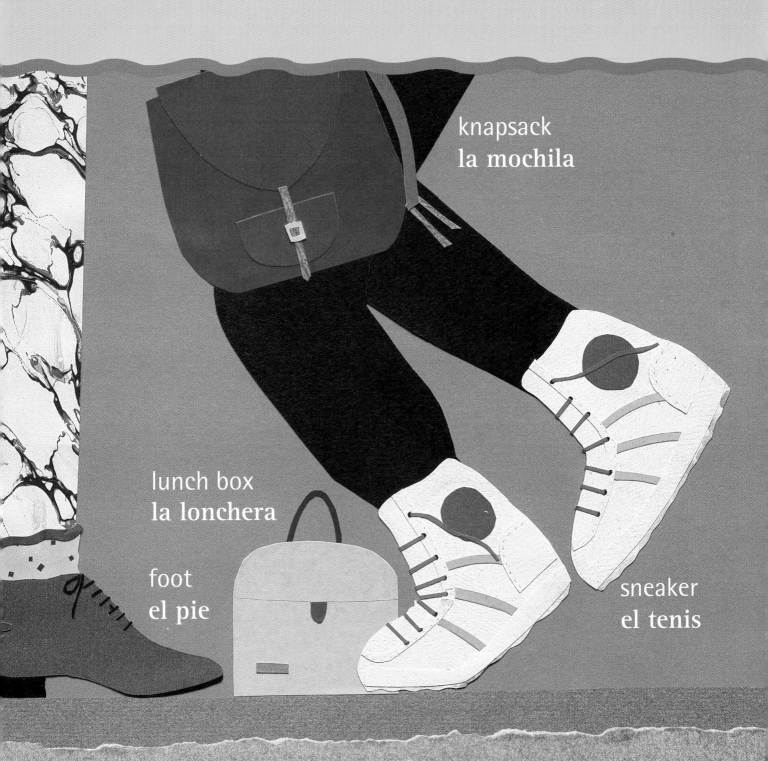

knapsack
la mochila

lunch box
la lonchera

foot
el pie

sneaker
el tenis

I carry my books and my lunch.
Llevo mis libros y mi almuerzo.

MY BEST FRIEND

This is my best friend, Jenny Lee. She is very smart. She plays the piano. I do, too. We like to go to the library together.

This is my best friend, Kathy Smith. She is very funny. She plays baseball. I do, too. We like to ride our bikes together.

Art Math Music
Science Social Studies
NGUAGE AR

Hey, My Friend

A Winter Soup Party

 LISTEN

 SPEAK

What has happened so far?

 THINK

What food do you think the animals are bringing to Little Donkey?

Self Holistic Portfolio
Traditional Performance
A S S E S S M E N T

Theme 1

 READ

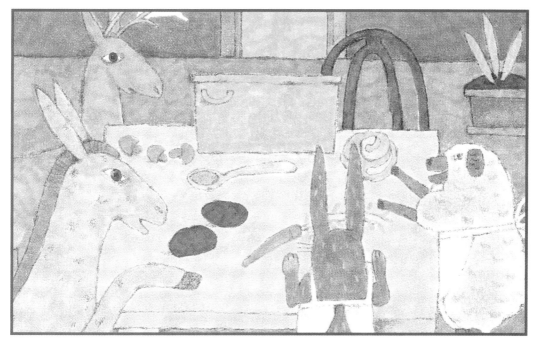

Little Rabbit has a carrot.

"We can put this in our soup," he says.

Little Sheep has a cabbage.

"We can put this in our soup," she says.

Little Doe has some mushrooms.

"We can put these in our soup," she says.

Little Donkey says, "I have some potatoes.

We can put them in our soup, too!"

They all help. And they all eat the delicious soup.

 THINK

Why was it cold?

 WRITE

Work with a partner and write a recipe for your own soup.

1. When is your birthday?
2. How many other kids were born in the same month?
3. Make a Class Birthday Graph and find out.

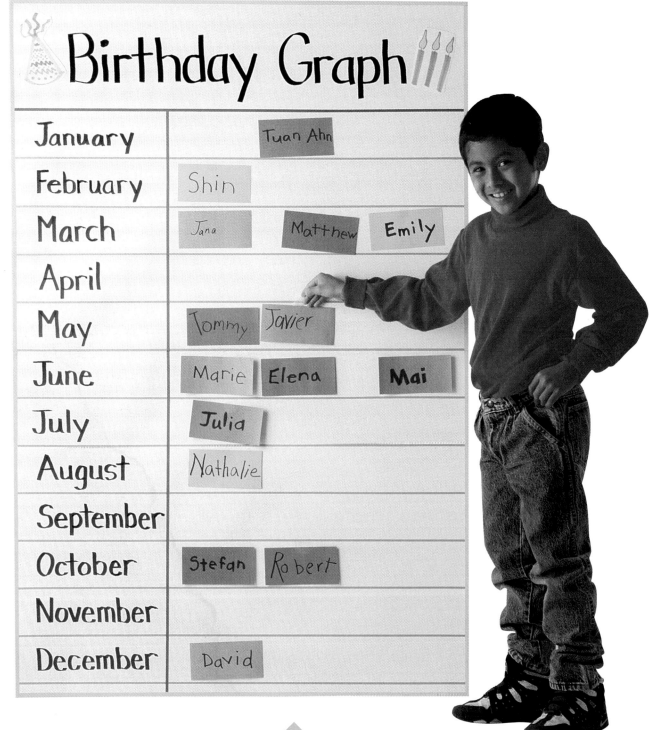

Birthday Graph

January	Tuan Ahn		
February	Shin		
March	Jana	Matthew	Emily
April			
May	Tommy	Javier	
June	Marie	Elena	Mai
July	Julia		
August	Nathalie		
September			
October	Stefan	Robert	
November			
December	David		

Art   Math   Music
Science   Social Studies
LANGUAGE ARTS

Family Times

I love you in the morning,
And in the afternoon.
I love you in the evening,
Underneath the moon.

My Aunt Came Back

Leader: My aunt came back

Everyone: My aunt came back

Leader: From old Japan

Everyone: From old Japan

Leader: And brought with her

Everyone: And brought with her

Leader: A lovely fan.

Everyone: A lovely fan.

My aunt came back
From Mexico,
And brought with her
A fine yo-yo.

Art Math Music
Science Social Studies
LANGUAGE ARTS

My aunt came back
From Guadeloupe,
And brought with her
A hoola hoop.

My aunt came back
From Niagara Falls,
And brought with her
Two soccer balls.

My aunt came back
From Timbuktu,
And brought with her
Some nuts to chew!

CRUNCH

CRUNCH

THE TREE BOY

BY NESLY BISSAINTHE

When I was small I lived in Haiti.
I did many things there that I liked a lot.
Right outside my house there was a
mango tree. I used to climb to the top
and eat mangoes with my friends.

Art | Math | Music
Science | Social Studies

LANGUAGE ARTS

Some people buy mangoes
in the market and bring the
mangoes back to their family.

It's fun for the whole family to eat mangoes together and tell stories. In my family, my grandparents would always tell stories.

20

TANGRAM TALES

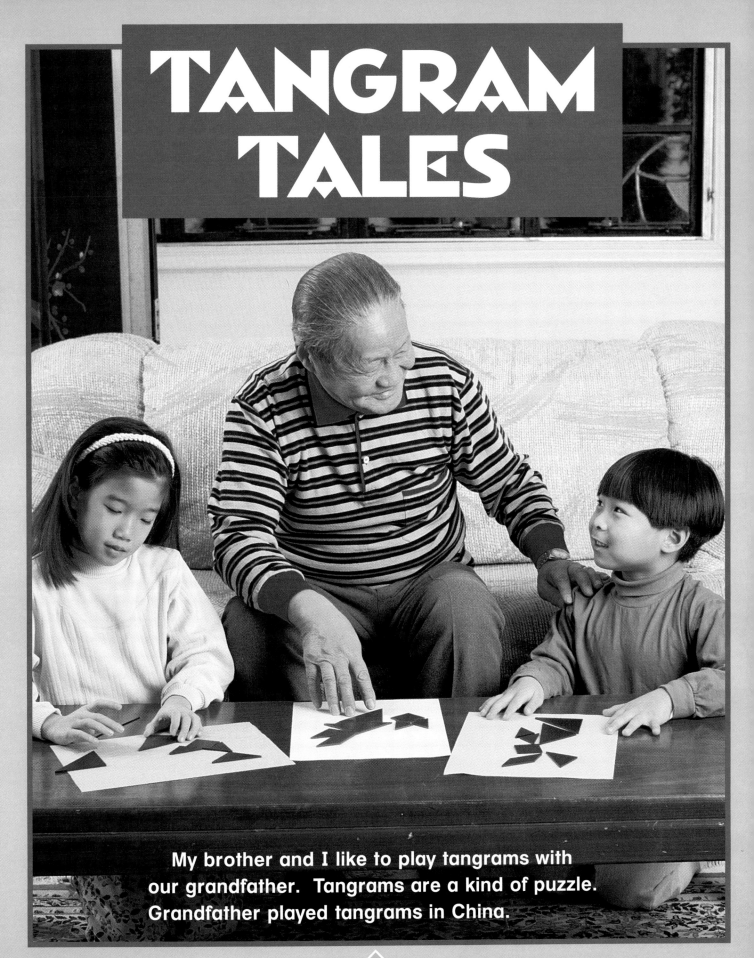

My brother and I like to play tangrams with
our grandfather. Tangrams are a kind of puzzle.
Grandfather played tangrams in China.

Art | Math | Music
Science | Social Studies
L A N G U A G E   A R T S

Grandfather tells us stories to go with the pictures. Some of the stories are about the Fox Fairy. The Fox Fairy can turn into many different animals. He can turn into a huge whale, or a little rabbit.

Fox

Rabbit

Sometimes my brother and I make up our own tangram pictures. Then we ask my parents and my grandfather to guess what they are.

Whale

What do you think this is?

OUR VACATION

Last year, we went to Boston in our van. My father drove. My mother sat beside him. My sister and I sat in the back. My parents said "Don't fight." That was funny. My sister and I fought all week.

Penguins!

We bought tickets to the aquarium. We saw penguins and fish. But we missed the dolphin show. We all felt sad.

The next day, we drove north. We stopped
at a pretty beach. We ate lunch there. After
lunch, we got a wonderful surprise.

We saw lots and lots of dolphins. They were
swimming and jumping and diving in the ocean.
"We didn't miss the dolphin show after all," said
my mom. We all felt glad.

How the Stars Got in the Sky

 LISTEN

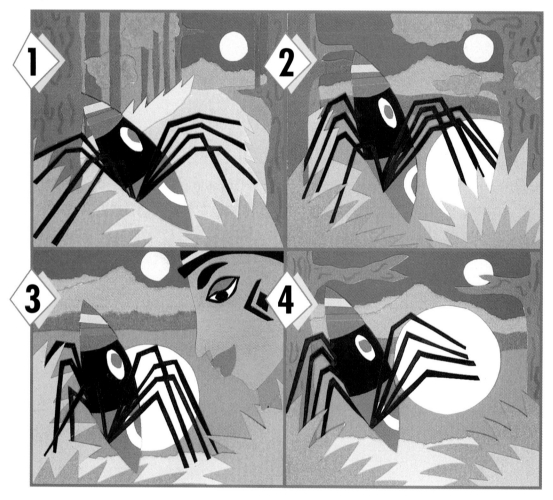

 SPEAK

What has happened so far?

 THINK

What will happen to the circle of light?

Self Holistic Portfolio
Traditional Performance
ASSESSMENT

Theme 2

READ

The circle of light hits the mountain.
It breaks into thousands of tiny pieces!
The pieces fly up into the sky.
Anansi looks up.
The sky is full of little white lights!
"How wonderful!" says Anansi.
That is how the stars got in the sky.

 ## THINK

Why didn't Anansi want to take the light home?

 ## WRITE

Make up a new story. Tell how birds or butterflies or
fireflies came to be.

What's the story behind your first name?
Talk to your family. Find out the story.

1. Who gave you your name?
2. Why did they choose
   that name?
3. Write down the story
   and make a name poster.

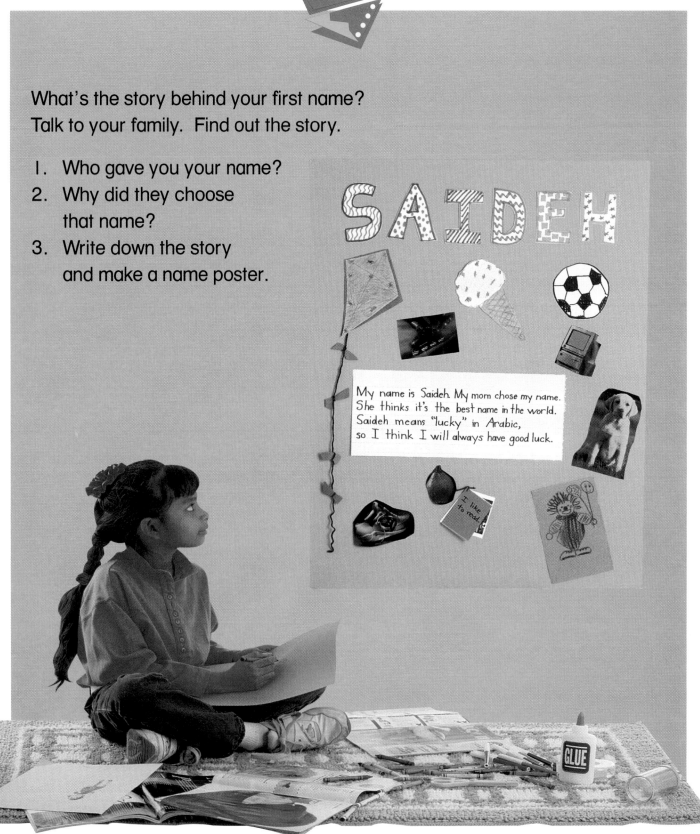

My name is Saideh. My mom chose my name.
She thinks it's the best name in the world.
Saideh means "lucky" in Arabic,
so I think I will always have good luck.

Art Math Music
Science Social Studies
LANGUAGE ARTS

Yes, I Can!

If you can walk you can dance.

If you can talk you can sing.

A saying from Africa

Terrific Tarah!

Tarah and her *Sesame Street* buddy, Prairie Dawn.

Tarah Lynne Schaeffer is nine years old. She lives in Connecticut. She works in New York City! Tarah is an actor on *Sesame Street*.

Art Math Music
Science Social Studies

LANGUAGE ARTS

Tarah has a disease called O. I. Her bones break easily, and she is much shorter than most kids her age. But Tarah lives a busy life.

Tarah waits backstage for her scenes in the show.

She really enjoys wheelchair sports.

"I like going to the meets," says Tarah. "It's fun, and I make lots of friends."

Tarah is in the lead as she races down the track.

Tarah and Luis *(Emilio Delgado)* dance together.

We asked Tarah, "Do you have something special to say to kids reading this article?"

"Yes," she said. "If you really want to do something— even if you don't think you can— just try! You have to believe in yourself."

"Believe in yourself!"

I Can

I can
be anything
I can
do anything
I can
think
anything
big
or tall
OR
high or low
W I D E
or narrow
fast or slow
because I
CAN
and
I
WANT
TO!

Mari Evans

Art Math Music
Science Social Studies

L a n g u a g e   A r t s

THE KNEE-HIGH MAN

AN AFRICAN-AMERICAN FOLKTALE

Characters:

Storyteller **Knee-High Man** **Horse** **Bull** **Owl**

Storyteller

Once there was a man no taller than a person's knee.
People called him the Knee-High Man.

Knee-High Man

I hate being so short. I want to get bigger.
Horse is the biggest animal I know.
Maybe Horse can tell me how to get big.

Art Math Music
Science Social Studies

Language Arts

 **Knee-High Man** Horse, how can I get big like you?

 Horse Well, eat a lot of corn. Then run and run as long as you can. Soon you'll be as big as me!

 **Storyteller** The Knee-High Man ate a lot of corn. Then he ran and ran until his legs hurt. But he didn't get any bigger.

 **Knee-High Man** Horse was wrong. I did just what he said, and I'm not any bigger. Bull is big. I'll go talk to him.

Yes, I Can!

 Knee-High Man Bull, how can I get big like you?

 **Bull** Eat a lot of grass. Then bellow and bellow as loud as you can. Soon you'll be as big as me!

 **Storyteller** The Knee-High Man ate a lot of grass. He bellowed and bellowed until his throat hurt. But he didn't get any bigger.

 **Knee-High Man** Bull was wrong. I did just what he said, and I'm not any bigger. Owl isn't big, but he is wise. Maybe he can tell me how to get big. I'll go talk to him.

Knee-High Man: Owl, how do I get to be as big as Horse and Bull?

Owl: Why do you want to be big?

Knee-High Man: I want to be big so that when I get into a fight, I will always win.

Owl: Have you ever been in a fight?

Knee-High Man: Well, no.

Yes, I Can!

Owl Then you don't need to be big.

Knee-High Man Yes I do! I need to be big so...so I can see far into the distance.

Owl Climb to the top of a tall tree. Then you can see far into the distance.

Knee-High Man Oh. I didn't think of that.

Owl Knee-High Man, you haven't done any thinking at all. You don't need to be as big as Horse or Bull. You're fine, just the way you are!

Storyteller So the Knee-High Man stopped worrying about being big. He was happy being just who he was.

THE SALT AND PEPPER SHAKE

1.

S and P

JAM and [bread]

Put your [hands]

On your [head/face]

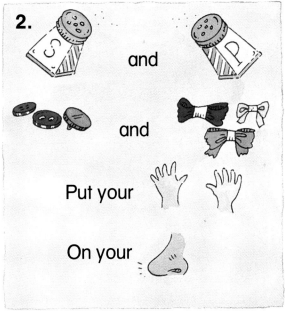

2.

S and P

[buttons] and [bows]

Put your [hands]

On your [nose]

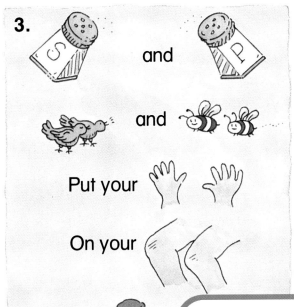

3.

S and P

[bird] and [bees]

Put your [hands]

On your [knees]

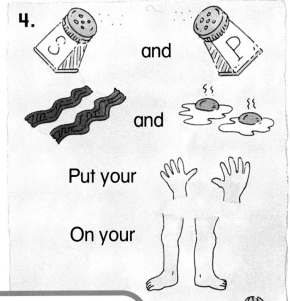

4.

S and P

[bacon] and [eggs]

Put your [hands]

On your [legs]

Shake, shake, shake!
Shake all around.
Shake your body up and down!

Art Math Music
Science Social Studies

L a n g u a g e   A r t s

Little Ant Helps Out

Listen

Speak

What has happened so far?

Think

What do you think Little Ant will do next?

Self Holistic Portfolio
Traditional Performance
Assessment

Theme 3

▶ **Read**

Little Ant called to her friend Little Bee.
"Please help me move the stone," said Little Ant.
"OK," said Little Bee.
Little Ant and Little Bee pushed and pushed. The stone
finally rolled off the stick.

"Mother Bluebird," said Little Ant, "you can pick up the
stick now."
Mother Bluebird picked up the stick.
"Thank you," she said to Little Ant and Little Bee. "You are
good friends."

▶ **Think**

Why did Mother Bluebird want the stick?

▶ **Write**

Imagine that Little Ant and Little Bee pushed and pushed
the stone, but it was too heavy. It did not move. What
could they do next? Write a new ending for the story.

HANDS-ON SCIENCE

Breaths in 1 minute

	Before jumping	After jumping
Deena	15	
Ben	17	

1. Count your breaths for one minute.
2. Jump 20 times. Count your breaths again.
3. What did you find out?

Art Math Music
Science Social Studies

Language Arts

Busy Days

Busy, busy, busy all the time.
Makes me feel dizzy
When I'm busy all the time.

"A" is for astronaut
"A" es por astronauta

Near Lorena Street School there is a long, concrete wall. Once, the wall was dirty and ugly. Now it is beautiful. Children, teachers, and parents all worked together to paint a wonderful mural.

Lorena Street Elementary School, Los Angeles, California

Art   Math   Music
Science   Social Studies
L A N G U A G E   A R T S

Mrs. Harder, a kindergarten teacher, started the mural. She drew a row of children dressed in the clothes of different occupations. She drew a person for each letter of the alphabet. All the children wanted to help paint big pictures on the wall.

"When you see you can be anything you want, like a doctor or a dentist, you feel good about yourself."
– David

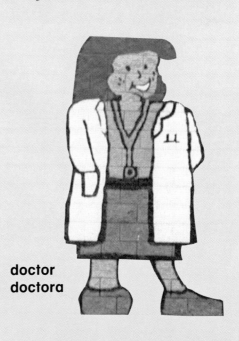

**doctor
doctora**

Most of the families in East Los Angeles speak Spanish. So the words on the mural are in both English and in Spanish. But there is room for other languages, too.

"Maybe new families will move to the neighborhood," says Mrs. Harder. "If they speak other languages, they can add their words, too."

Everybody is proud of the mural. Mrs. Harder says, "I always tell my students, "You can do anything. You can be anything."

ecologist
ecologista

"People think about the hard work we all did, and they are proud. It changed the neighborhood."
-Gustavo

Presents for America

Long ago, a man named John Chapman lived in the
state of Massachusetts. He loved the outdoors.

One day, he was walking in the woods. He stopped to rest
and to eat an apple. Afterwards, he looked at the apple seeds
in his hands.

Art Math Music
Science Social Studies
LANGUAGE ARTS

"I'm going to plant these seeds," he said to himself. "I'm going to plant many, many seeds all over America. Our land will soon be filled with apple trees." And that is just what he did.

Busy Days

He started a long journey. He carried a bag of apple seeds on his back. He walked north. He walked south. He walked east. He walked west.

He planted apple seeds everywhere he went.

John Chapman gave apple seeds to everyone
he met. Soon, everyone called him Johnny Appleseed.

Today, we can still see some of the trees that Johnny
Appleseed planted. They are large, old trees filled with apples.
They are the presents he gave to his country.

Balloons for Sale

● ● ● ● ● ● ● ● ● ● ● ● ●

▶ **LISTEN**

▶ **SPEAK**

What has happened so far?

▶ **THINK**

What do you think Pig will say?

Self Holistic Portfolio
Traditional Performance
A S S E S S M E N T

Theme 4

READ

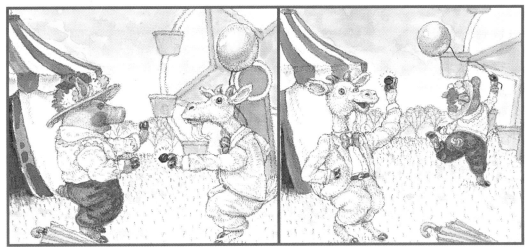

"Oh, my," says Pig. "I don't want to buy a broken balloon."

"Here is your penny back," says Goat sadly.

"Oh, no," says Pig. "You can keep my penny. Please give me the yellow balloon!"

Goat gives Pig the yellow balloon.
Pig puts her umbrella down.
She dances away with the beautiful yellow balloon.
"Thank you, Goat," she says.
"You're welcome," says Goat.

 ## THINK

How many pennies does Goat have?

 ## WRITE

What else can make a balloon pop? Draw or write some ideas.

HANDS-ON SCIENCE

A magnet can pull many things.
Feel the pull of a magnet.
What can your magnet pull?

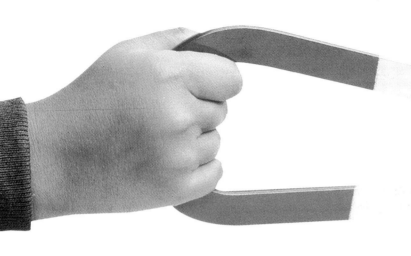

Try these things.		YES	NO
a penny			
paper clips			
scissors			
pencils			
a dime			
a string			
a crayon			
paper			
a jar lid			

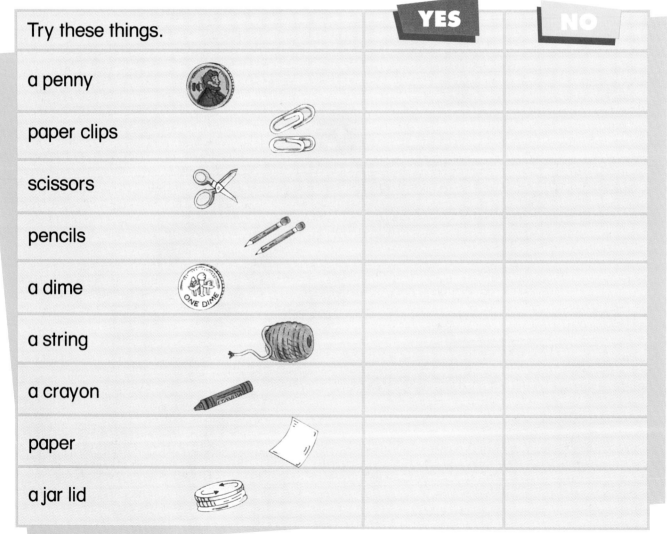

Art Math Music
Science Social Studies
L A N G U A G E   A R T S

Around the Pond

In August when the days are hot,
I like to find a shady spot,
And hardly move a bit—
And sit—
And sit—
And sit—
And sit!

Why Rabbits Have Short Tails

AN AFRICAN-AMERICAN FOLKTALE

Once upon a time, rabbits had short ears and fine long tails.

Now, rabbits have long ears and short fluffy tails.

This is how it happened.

One cold winter day, Rabbit met a Fox. Fox was carrying a long string of fish.

"Where did you get those fish?" asked Rabbit.

"From the pond," said Fox.

"But it's winter," said Rabbit. "The pond is covered with ice."

"Yes, but I know a trick," said Fox. "Come with me and I'll show you."

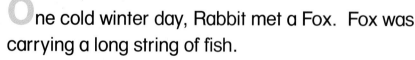

LANGUAGE ARTS

Rabbit followed Fox down to the pond. Fox showed Rabbit a hole in the ice.

Fox said, "Sit here on the ice. Let your fine long tail hang down into the water. Stay here all night. In the morning you'll have a string of fish on your tail."

So Rabbit sat on the ice. He let his fine long tail hang down into the water. He sat and sat and sat all night. It was very cold and very uncomfortable, but Rabbit kept thinking of the wonderful fried fish he would have for breakfast.

Finally, morning came. "It's time to pull up my fish!" said Rabbit. Rabbit tried to stand up, but his tail was frozen in the ice! "Help, help! I'm stuck!" cried Rabbit.

Owl heard Rabbit. She came to help. "I will pull you by your ears," said Owl. "Then you will not be stuck."

Owl pulled Rabbit by his ears. She pulled and pulled. Rabbit's ears got longer and longer, but he was still stuck in the ice.

"I think we need more help," said Owl.

All Rabbit's friends came down to the pond to help. They pulled and pulled and pulled. Finally, Rabbit was free, but his fine long tail stayed in the ice. All that remained was a short fluffy cotton tail.

That is why today all rabbits have long ears and short tails. And whenever they see a fox, they run the other way!

THE LITTLE TURTLE

There was a little turtle.
He lived in a box.
He swam in a puddle.
He climbed the rocks.

He snapped at a mosquito.
He snapped at a flea.
He snapped at a minnow.
And he snapped at me.

He caught the mosquito.
He caught the flea.
He caught the minnow.
But he didn't catch me.

Vachel Lindsey

Art Math Music
Science Social Studies
LANGUAGE ARTS

BUSY BEAVERS

Beavers build their homes from trees. They chew down the trees with their big front teeth.

A beaver's home is called a lodge. Beavers build their lodges in the middle of ponds.

The lodges have mud floors. The beavers eat and sleep on the mud floor.

Art Math Music
Science Social Studies

LANGUAGE ARTS

Beavers eat leaves and tree bark. They store tree branches at the bottom of the pond. These branches are food for the winter.

When the top of the pond freezes over, beavers bring the branches into their lodge. If all the pond freezes, beavers still have food. They eat the walls of their lodge!

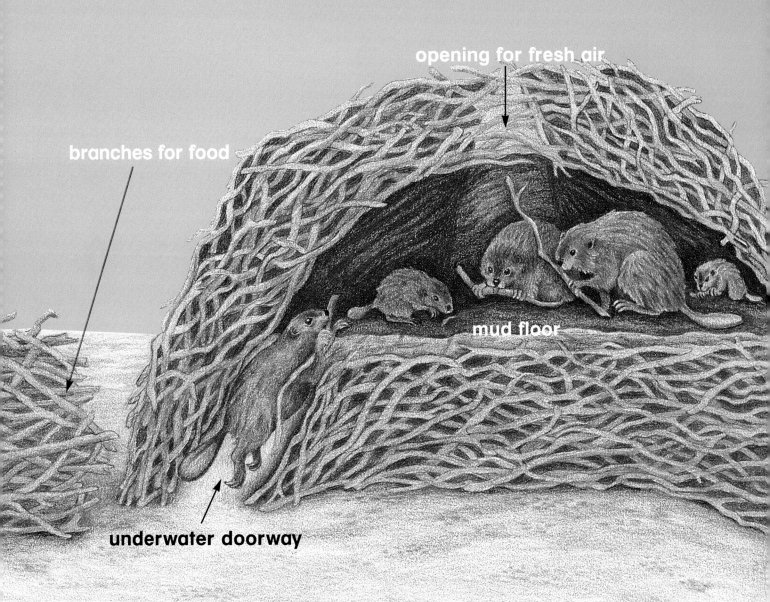

opening for fresh air

branches for food

mud floor

underwater doorway

Beavers are good swimmers. Baby beavers learn how to swim when they are only a few days old. When a beaver sees danger, it slaps its wide tail against the water. That makes a loud noise. The other beavers dive quickly under the water. They are safe in their lodge.

Beavers talk to each other. They rub noses, make soft sounds, and whistle.

The coquí is a tiny tree frog that lives in the rain forests of Puerto Rico. Every evening, around sunset, the coquíes sing a song.

El Coquí

A LULLABY FROM PUERTO RICO

El Coquí sings a sweet song at twilight.
He is singing as sleep comes to me.
When I wake all alone in the moonlight,
El Coquí sings good night from the tree.

Coquí, Coquí, Coquí, quí, quí, quí,
Coquí, Coquí, Coquí, quí, quí, quí.

Around the Pond

Art Math Music
Science Social Studies

CLASSES UNDER THE TREES

BY MONICA GUNNING   PICTURES BY FRANÉ LESSAC

My teacher, Miss Zettie, says,
"Children, we can't breathe in here.
Come on! We're going
under the breadfruit tree!"

We leave the one room schoolhouse
these hot days in June
for the breeze outdoors
below blue skies.

Reciting our lessons
in singsong fashion,
we hear twittering birds
recite theirs, too.

Nature Walk

The Ungrateful Tiger

A FOLKTALE FROM KOREA

CHARACTERS:

| Storyteller | Tree | Tiger | Ox | Man | Rabbit |

Storyteller

A long time ago, a tiger was walking through the jungle. Suddenly, he fell into a deep pit.

Tiger

Help, help! Get me out of this pit!

Storyteller

Nobody heard the tiger. Nobody came to help. Many days passed. Finally, a man came down the jungle path.

Tiger

Please, please help me!

Man

I'm sorry, but I can't help you. If I do, you'll eat me up.

Tiger

No, no, I won't. I promise I won't. I'll be grateful to you forever.

Storyteller

The man found a long tree branch, and dropped it into the pit. The tiger climbed up the branch.

Tiger

That's better. Say, you look quite delicious, and I'm starving!

Man

Wait a minute! You promised you wouldn't eat me.

Tiger

Yes, but I didn't realize how hungry I was.

Man

That's not fair! I just saved your life. You can't eat me! That would be very ungrateful. Tree, don't you agree with me?

Tree

We trees give you shade and fruit to eat. But you cut us down for lumber. Ungrateful—ha! Tiger, enjoy your lunch!

Nature Walk

Man

Wait, wait. Here's an ox.
Ox, don't you agree with me?

Ox

We oxen work hard for you. We carry heavy loads
and plow your land. But when we get old, you kill us
for food. Ungrateful—ha! Tiger, enjoy your lunch.

Man

Wait, wait. Here comes a rabbit. Let's hear what the rabbit says.

Storyteller

The tiger and the man told the rabbit their story. The rabbit listened
very carefully. She stroked her long ears and twitched her nose.

Rabbit

I think I need to see the pit and hear the story again. Lead the way...Now, let me make sure I understand. Tiger, you were up here and the man was in the pit?

Tiger

No, no, that's not right. I was in the pit—like this.

Storyteller

The tiger jumped into the deep pit. The man and the rabbit stared down at the tiger.

Rabbit

The man helped you get out, right?

Tiger

Yes, but...

Rabbit

And in return, you promised not to eat him, right?

Tiger

Yes, but…

Rabbit

And you broke your promise, right?

Tiger

Yes, but…

Rabbit

No "buts" about it, Tiger. You will stay in the pit. The man will go on his way— and so will I.

Storyteller

The tiger roared and roared, deep down in the pit. Then a crow flew by…but that's another story for another time.

Put some seeds in a jar with paper.
Add some water.

SUN	MON	TUES	WED	THURS	FRI	SAT

SPROUT

Wait for the
seeds to sprout.
Mark each day
you wait
on the calendar.

How many days
did it take?

Do all seeds take
the same time?

Seasons, Seasons Everywhere!

 LISTEN

UNITED STATES	AUSTRALIA
1	
2	
3	

 SPEAK

What has happened so far?

 THINK

What season will come next in the United States?

What season will come next in Australia?

Theme **6**

 READ

| UNITED STATES | AUSTRALIA |

The children said, "It's winter! Let's make a snowman."
They rolled the snow into big balls.
They made a tall snowman. They gave him a hat!

On the same day in Australia, it was summer.
What were the children doing in Australia?
Petting kangaroos at the zoo and sailing on a lake.

 THINK

Could children in the United States see kangaroos
in the summer?

 WRITE

What is your favorite season? What do you like to do
then? Draw and write your answer.

INDEX